T0300682

ED EMBERLEY'S
Drawing Book
MAKE A WORLD

LITTLE, BROWN & COMPANY
LB kids

THIS BOOK WILL SHOW YOU
HOW TO DRAW ENOUGH THINGS
TO MAKE A WORLD OF YOUR OWN.
I HOPE YOU WILL TRY THIS WAY,
CONTINUE TO DRAW YOUR OWN WAY,
AND KEEP LOOKING FOR NEW WAYS—
I DO.

Happy Drawing!
Ed Emberley

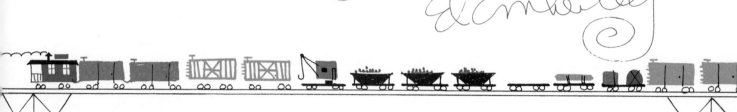

Text and illustrations by Edward R. Emberley
Text and illustrations copyright © 1972, 2006 by International Literary Properties LLC

Cover illustration by Edward R. Emberley
Cover illustration copyright © 2006 by International Literary Properties LLC
Cover copyright © 2006 by Hachette Book Group, Inc.

Little, Brown and Company
Hachette Book Group
1290 Avenue of the Americas, New York, NY 10104
Visit us at LBYR.com

Originally published in hardcover by Little, Brown and Company in March 1972
First Revised Paperback Edition: April 2006

LB kids is an imprint of Little, Brown and Company. The LB kids name and logo are trademarks of Hachette Book Group, Inc.

The publisher is not responsible for websites (or their content) that are not owned by the publisher.

Little, Brown and Company books may be purchased in bulk for business, educational, or promotional use. For information, please contact your local bookseller or the Hachette Book Group Special Markets Department at specialmarkets@hbgusa.com.

LCCN 2006277147

ISBN 978-0-316-78972-1

PRINTED IN CHINA

APS

30 29 28 27 26 25 24 23 22

IF YOU CAN DRAW THESE THINGS ——→
YOU CAN DRAW ALL THE OBJECTS
IN THIS BOOK.   FOR, INSTANCE:
YOU USE THESE   ◗ ▲ ▲ " " · |
TO MAKE THIS FISH   ▸◉
THE DIAGRAMS ON THE
FOLLOWING PAGES WILL SHOW
YOU HOW.

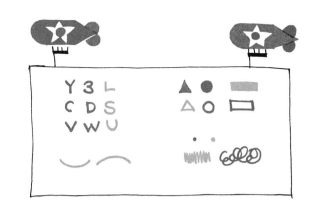

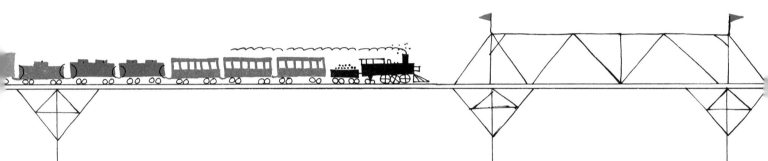

THE ARTWORK FOR THIS
BOOK WAS DRAWN ON
STRATHMORE PAPER
WITH FELT TIP AND
RAPIDOGRAPH PENS,
FOUR-COLOR, PRESEPARATED
AND HAND-LETTERED
BY THE AUTHOR.

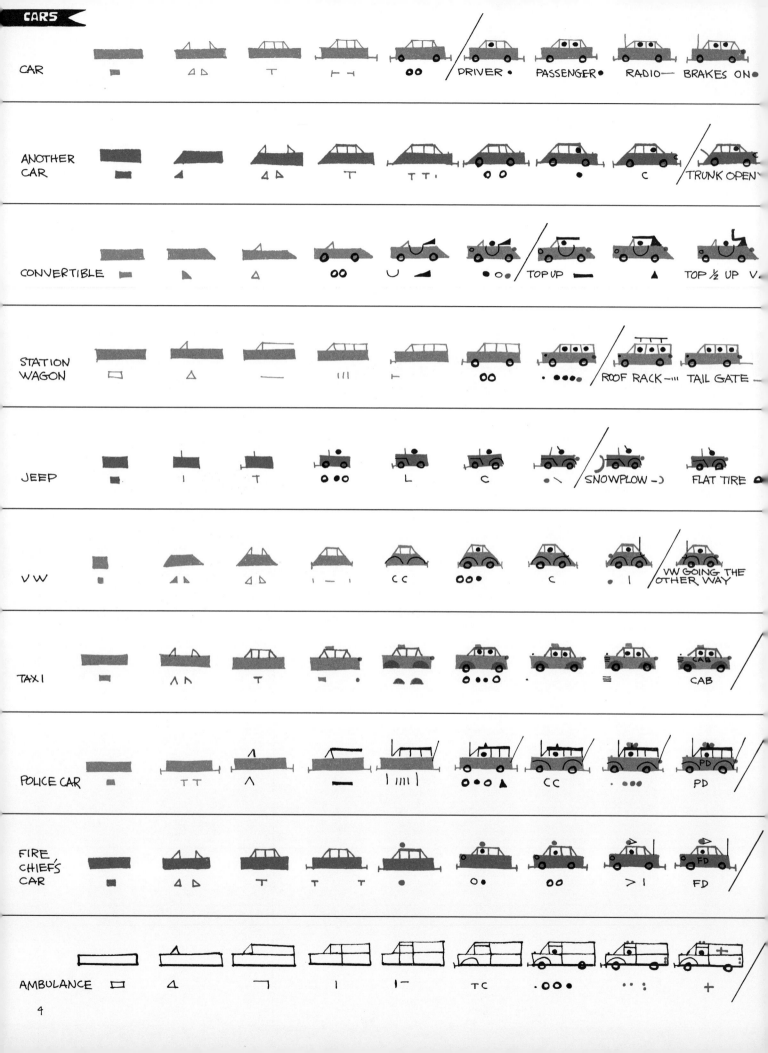

CAR

DRIVER • PASSENGER • RADIO — BRAKES ON •

ANOTHER CAR

TRUNK OPEN

CONVERTIBLE

TOP UP ▬ ▲ TOP ½ UP V.

STATION WAGON

ROOF RACK —''' TAIL GATE —

JEEP

SNOWPLOW —) FLAT TIRE

VW

VW GOING THE OTHER WAY

TAXI

CAB

POLICE CAR

PD

FIRE CHIEF'S CAR

FD

AMBULANCE

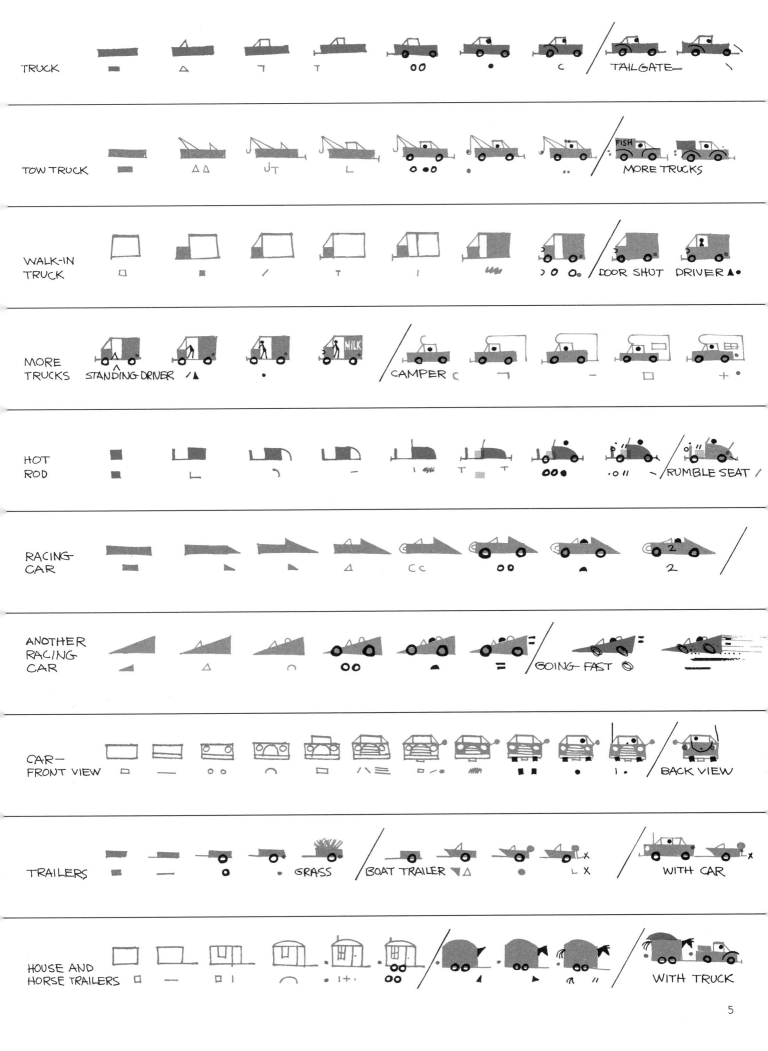

TRUCK

TOW TRUCK

WALK-IN TRUCK

MORE TRUCKS — STANDING DRIVER

HOT ROD

RACING CAR

ANOTHER RACING CAR

CAR — FRONT VIEW

TRAILERS

HOUSE AND HORSE TRAILERS

TAILGATE

MORE TRUCKS

DOOR SHUT   DRIVER

CAMPER

RUMBLE SEAT

GOING FAST

BACK VIEW

GRASS   BOAT TRAILER   WITH CAR

WITH TRUCK

5

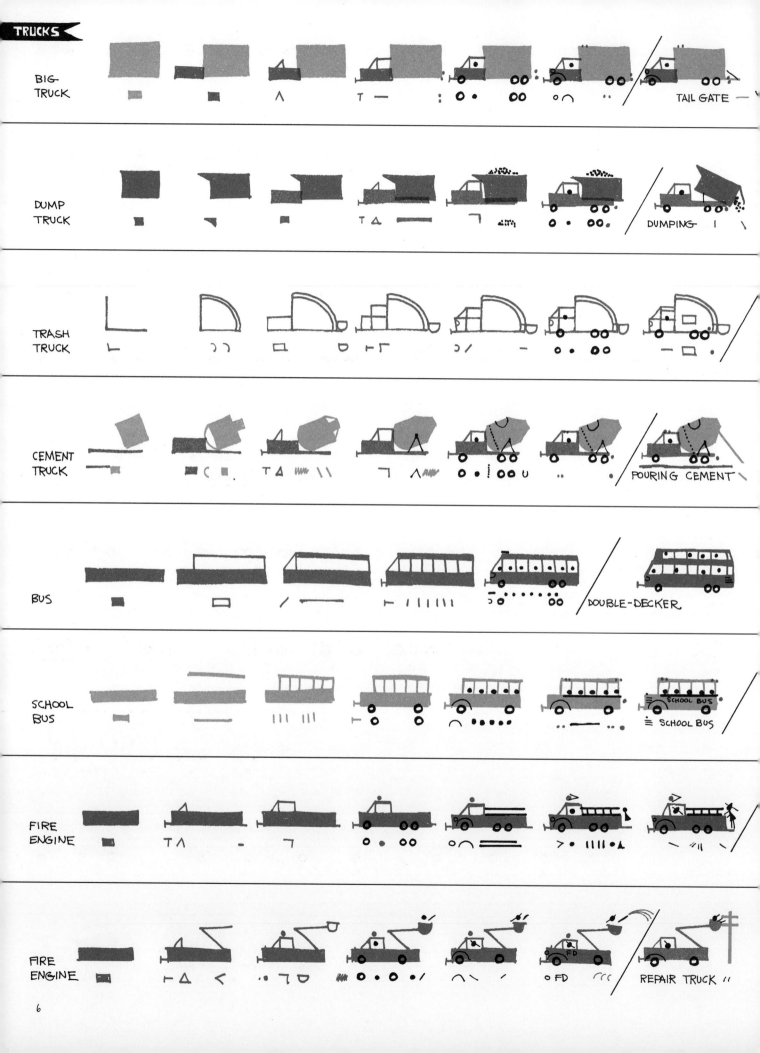

BIG TRUCK

DUMP TRUCK — DUMPING

TRASH TRUCK

CEMENT TRUCK — POURING CEMENT

BUS — DOUBLE-DECKER

SCHOOL BUS — SCHOOL BUS

FIRE ENGINE

FIRE ENGINE — REPAIR TRUCK

TAIL GATE

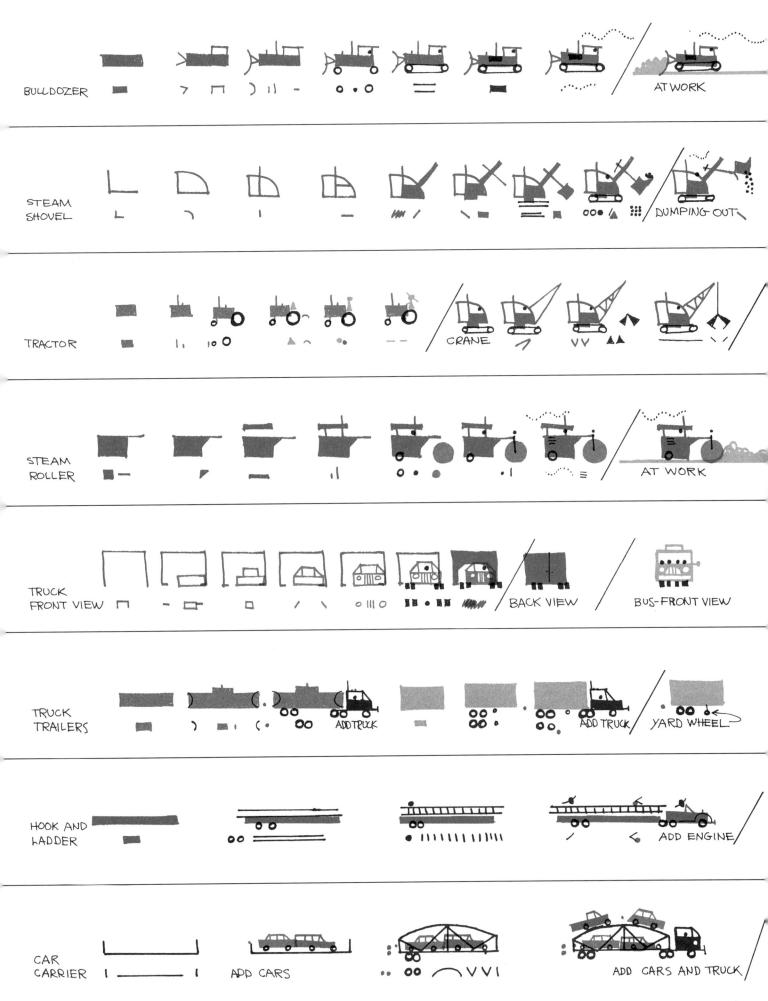

BULLDOZER

STEAM SHOVEL — DUMPING OUT

TRACTOR — CRANE

STEAM ROLLER — AT WORK

TRUCK FRONT VIEW — BACK VIEW — BUS-FRONT VIEW

TRUCK TRAILERS — ADD TRUCK — ADD TRUCK — YARD WHEEL

HOOK AND LADDER — ADD ENGINE

CAR CARRIER — ADD CARS — ADD CARS AND TRUCK

AT WORK

7

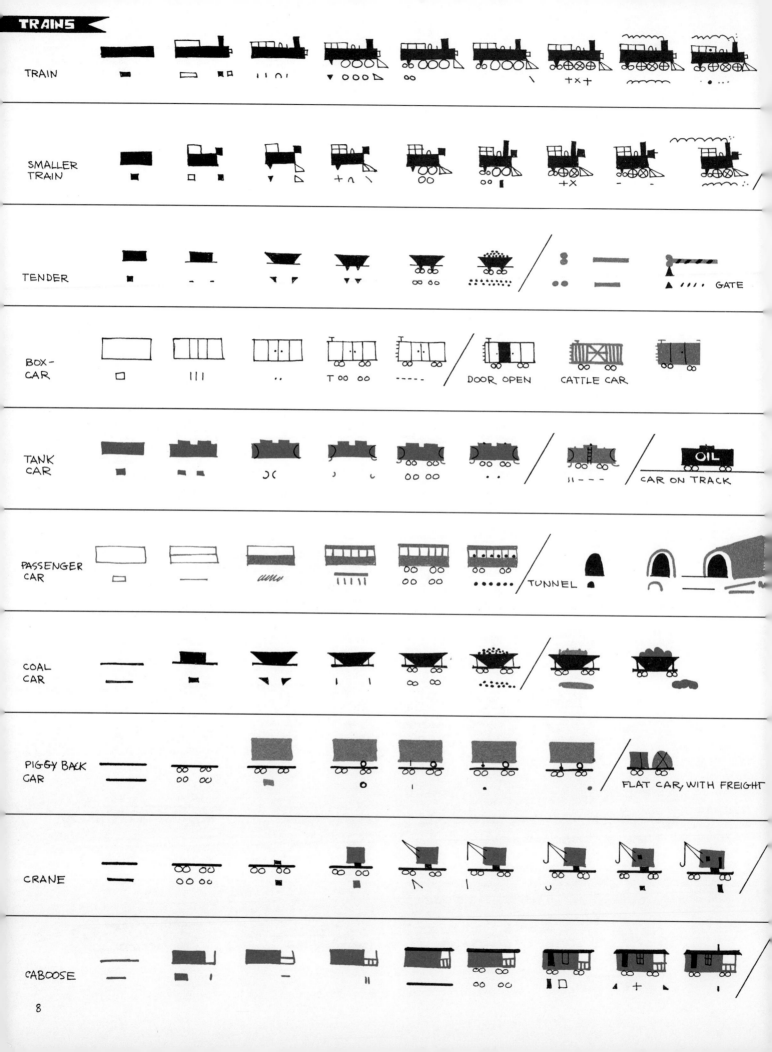

TRAIN

SMALLER TRAIN

TENDER — GATE

BOX-CAR — DOOR OPEN — CATTLE CAR

TANK CAR — OIL — CAR ON TRACK

PASSENGER CAR — TUNNEL

COAL CAR

PIGGY BACK CAR — FLAT CAR, WITH FREIGHT

CRANE

CABOOSE

8

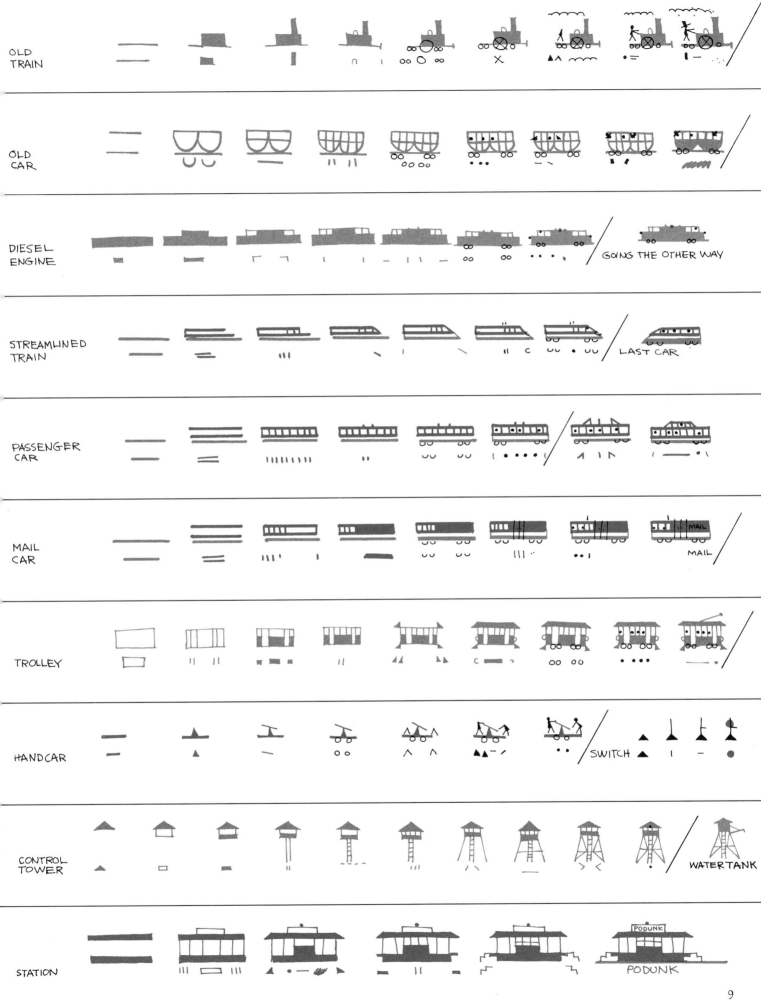

OLD TRAIN

OLD CAR

DIESEL ENGINE — GOING THE OTHER WAY

STREAMLINED TRAIN — LAST CAR

PASSENGER CAR

MAIL CAR — MAIL

TROLLEY

HANDCAR — SWITCH

CONTROL TOWER — WATERTANK

STATION — PODUNK

9

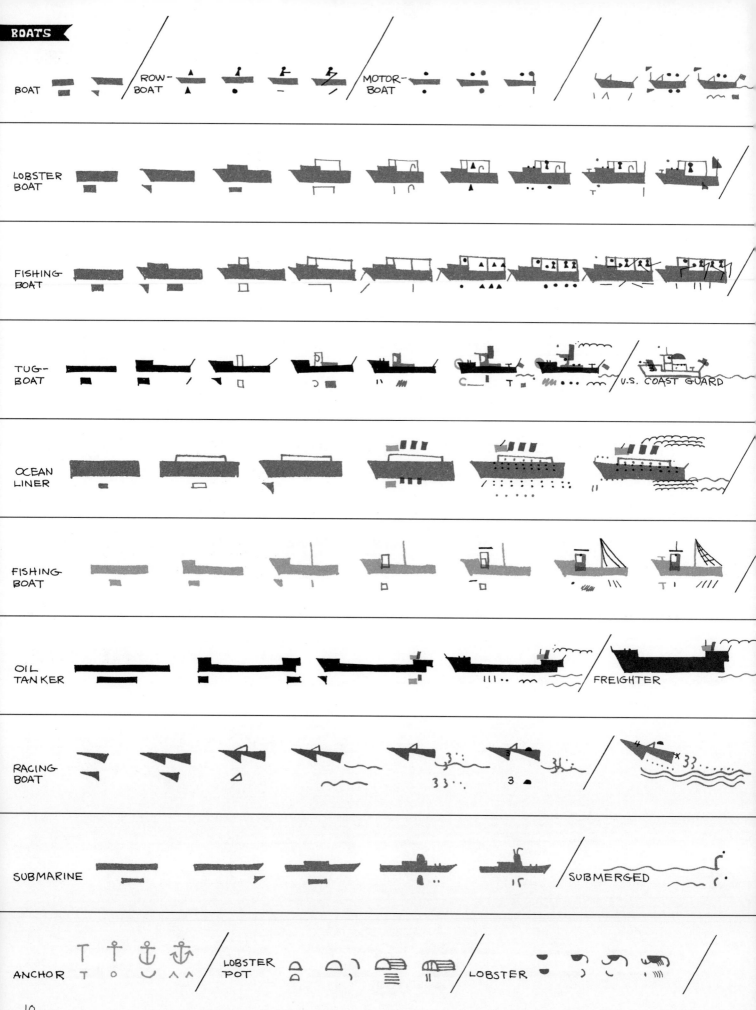

BOAT

ROW-BOAT

MOTOR-BOAT

LOBSTER BOAT

FISHING BOAT

TUG-BOAT

U.S. COAST GUARD

OCEAN LINER

FISHING BOAT

OIL TANKER

FREIGHTER

RACING BOAT

SUBMARINE

SUBMERGED

ANCHOR

LOBSTER POT

LOBSTER

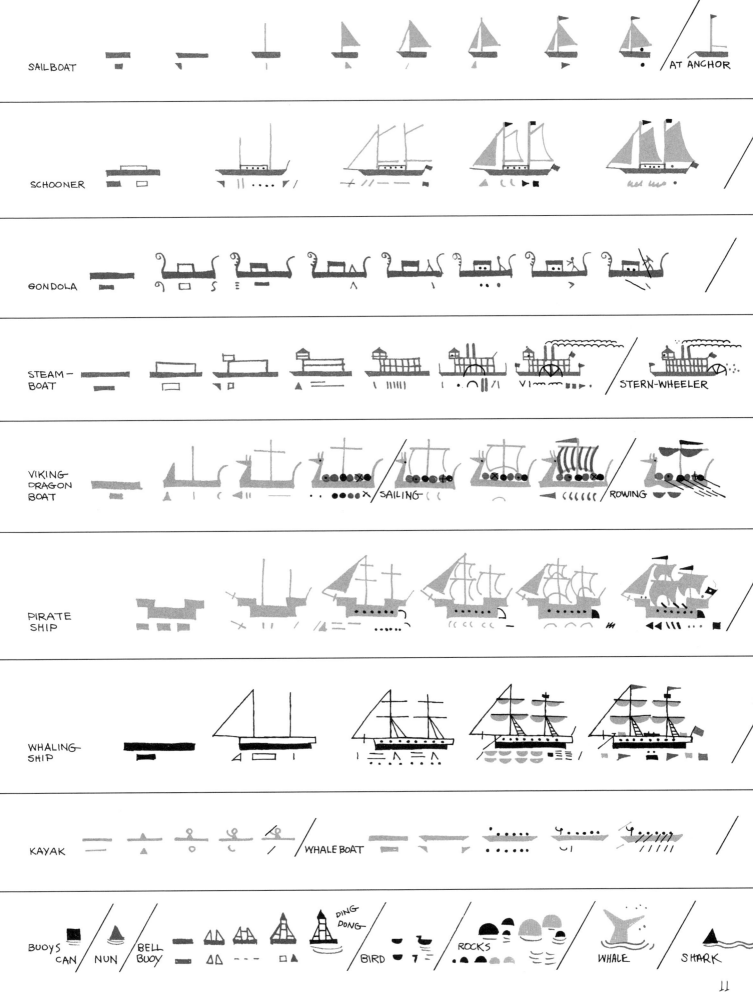

SAILBOAT

AT ANCHOR

SCHOONER

GONDOLA

STEAM-
BOAT

STERN-WHEELER

VIKING
DRAGON
BOAT

SAILING

ROWING

PIRATE
SHIP

WHALING
SHIP

KAYAK

WHALE BOAT

BUOYS
CAN

NUN

BELL
BUOY

DING
DONG

BIRD

ROCKS

WHALE

SHARK

11

OTHER VEHICLES

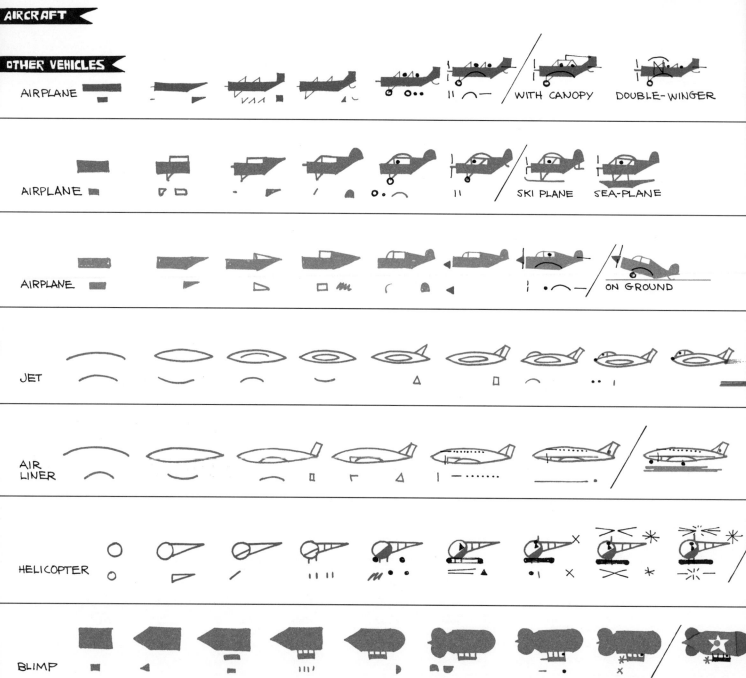

AIRPLANE ... WITH CANOPY ... DOUBLE-WINGER

AIRPLANE ... SKI PLANE ... SEA-PLANE

AIRPLANE ... ON GROUND

JET

AIR LINER

HELICOPTER

BLIMP

PARACHUTE

BALLOON

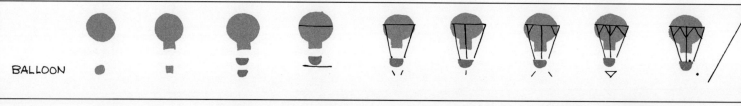

FRONT VIEWS

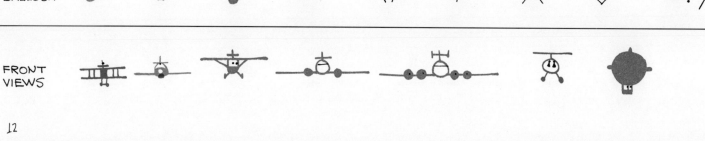

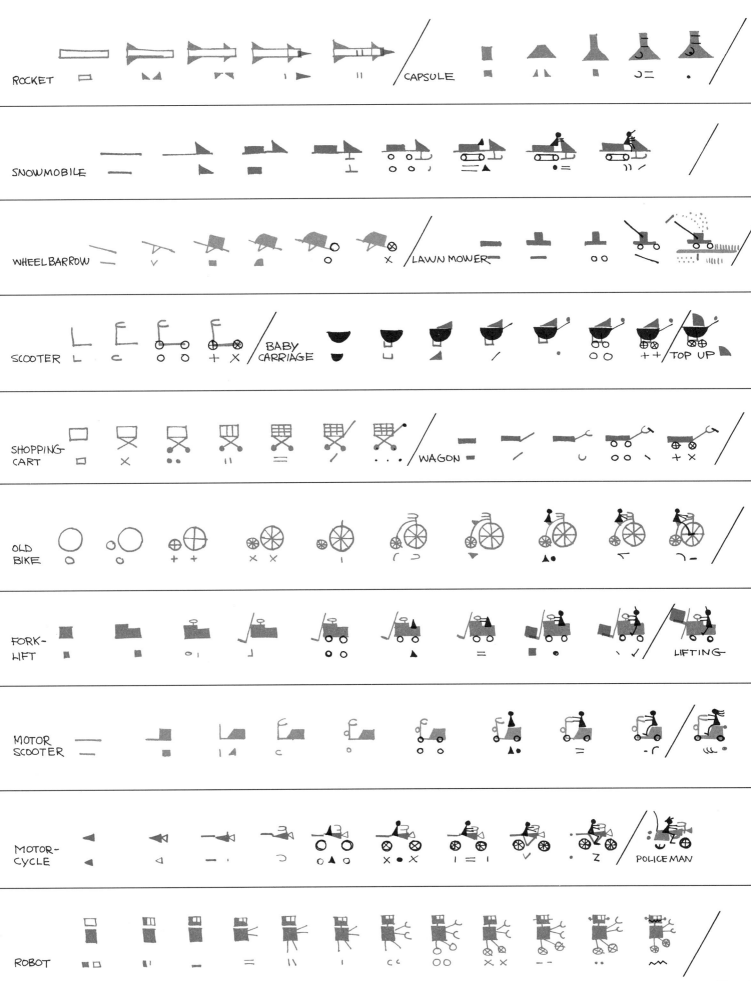

ROCKET

CAPSULE

SNOWMOBILE

WHEELBARROW

LAWN MOWER

SCOOTER

BABY CARRIAGE

TOP UP

SHOPPING CART

WAGON

OLD BIKE

FORK-LIFT

LIFTING

MOTOR SCOOTER

MOTOR-CYCLE

POLICEMAN

ROBOT

13

HORSE

HORSE
WALKING

HORSE
RUNNING

HORSE
RUNNING

HORSE
JUMPING

EATING

DONKEY

DEER

CAMEL

CAMEL

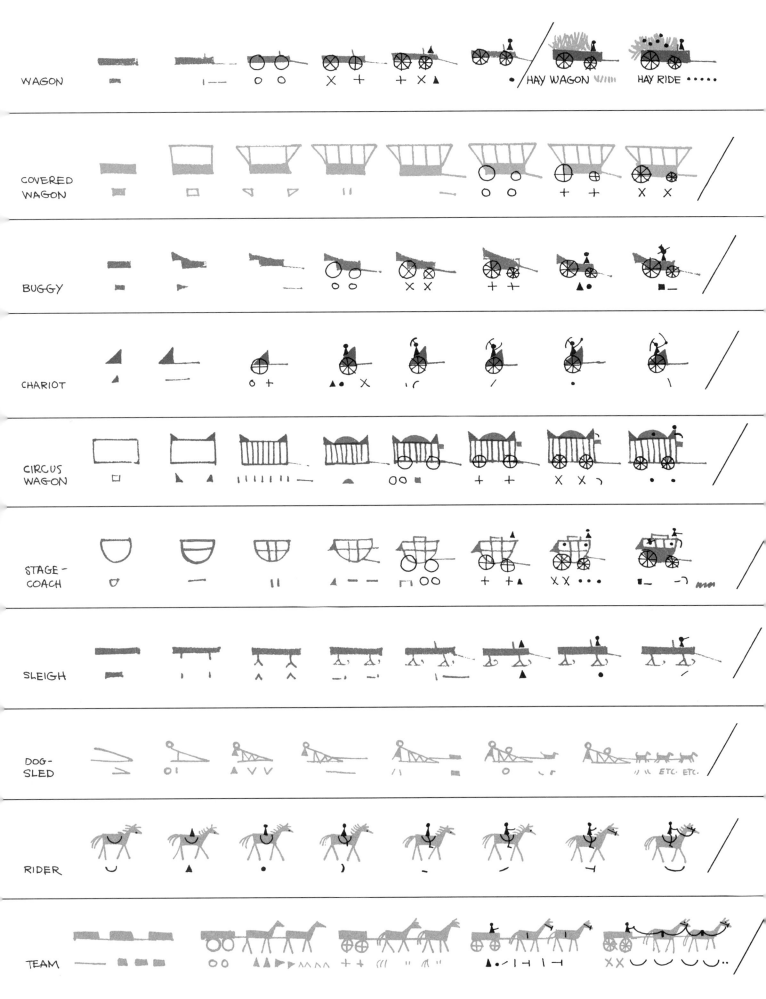

WAGON

COVERED WAGON

BUGGY

CHARIOT

CIRCUS WAGON

STAGE-COACH

SLEIGH

DOG-SLED

RIDER

TEAM

HAY WAGON

HAY RIDE

ETC. ETC.

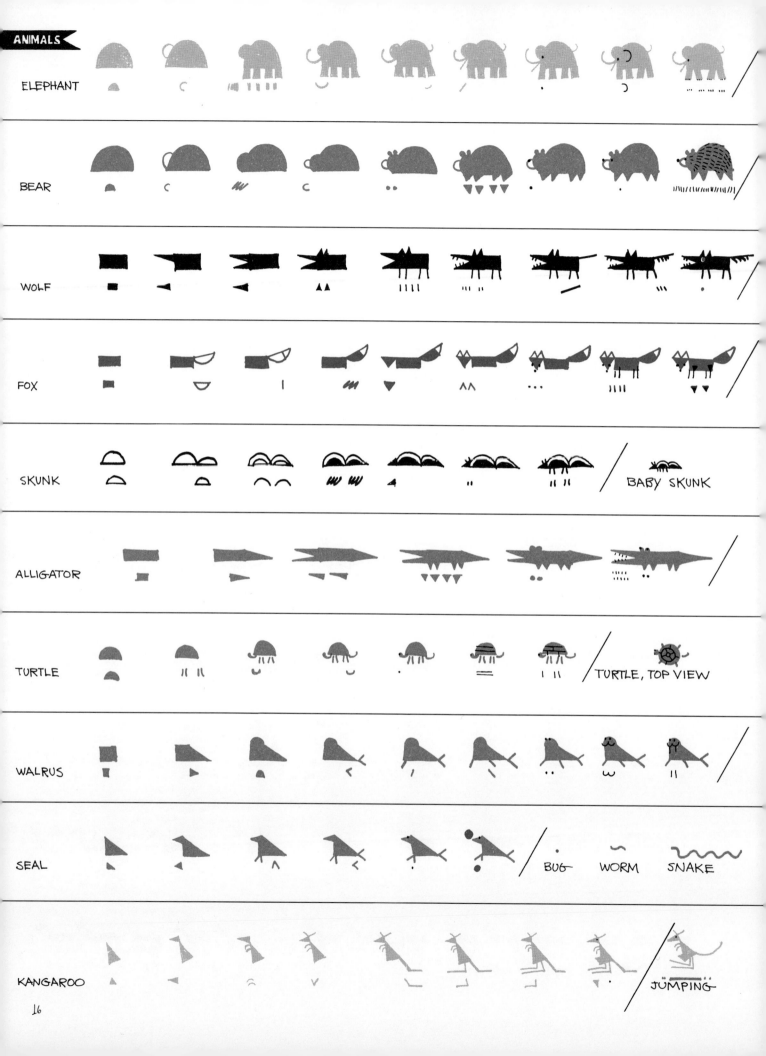

ELEPHANT

BEAR

WOLF

FOX

SKUNK   BABY SKUNK

ALLIGATOR

TURTLE   TURTLE, TOP VIEW

WALRUS

SEAL   BUG   WORM   SNAKE

KANGAROO   JUMPING

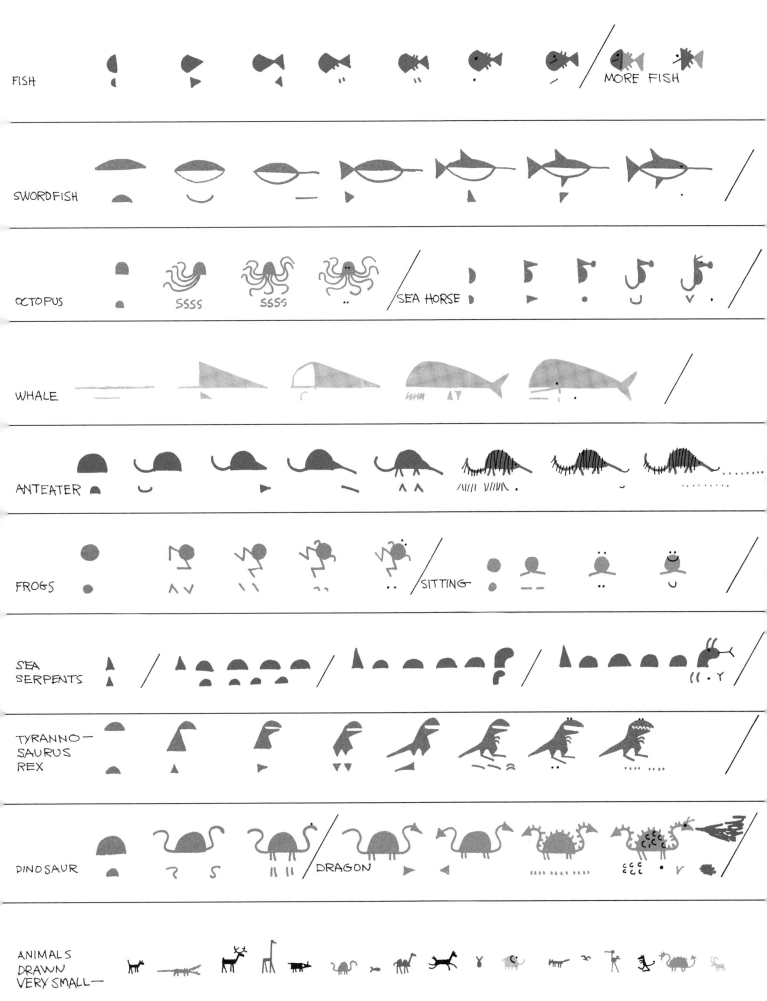

FISH

SWORDFISH

OCTOPUS

SEA HORSE

WHALE

ANTEATER

FROGS

SITTING

SEA
SERPENTS

TYRANNO-
SAURUS
REX

DINOSAUR

DRAGON

ANIMALS
DRAWN
VERY SMALL—

MORE FISH

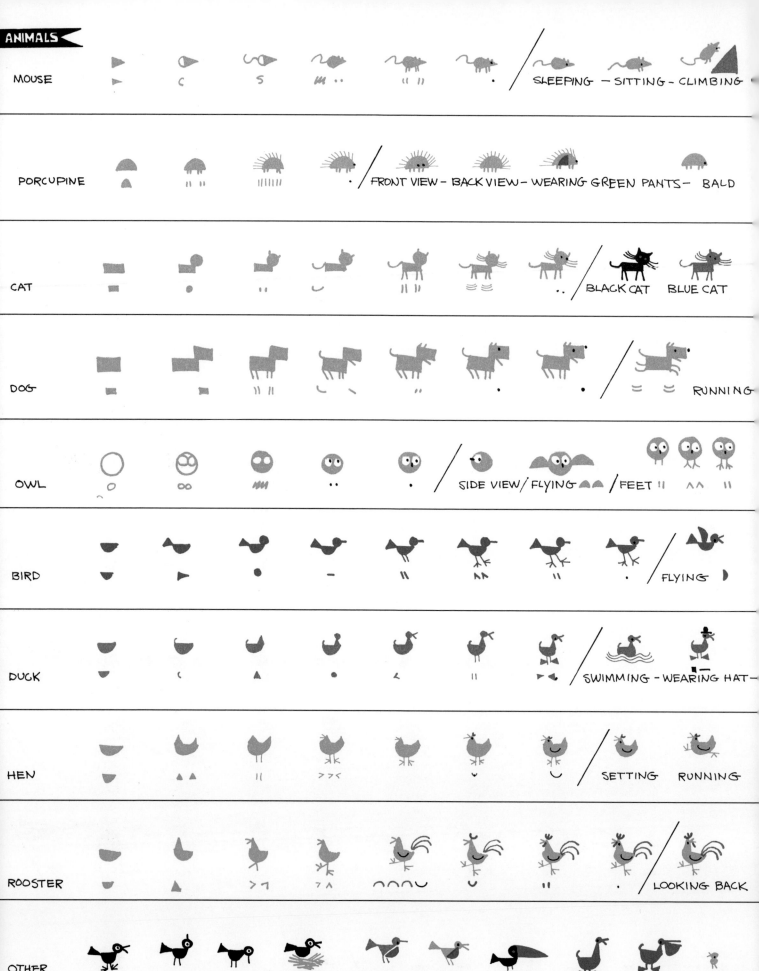

MOUSE — SLEEPING — SITTING — CLIMBING

PORCUPINE — FRONT VIEW — BACK VIEW — WEARING GREEN PANTS — BALD

CAT — BLACK CAT — BLUE CAT

DOG — RUNNING

OWL — SIDE VIEW / FLYING / FEET

BIRD — FLYING

DUCK — SWIMMING — WEARING HAT —

HEN — SETTING — RUNNING

ROOSTER — LOOKING BACK

OTHER BIRDS — CROW — LOOKING UP — PECKING — NESTING — BLUE BIRD — ROBIN — TOUCAN — GOOSE — PELICAN — CHICK

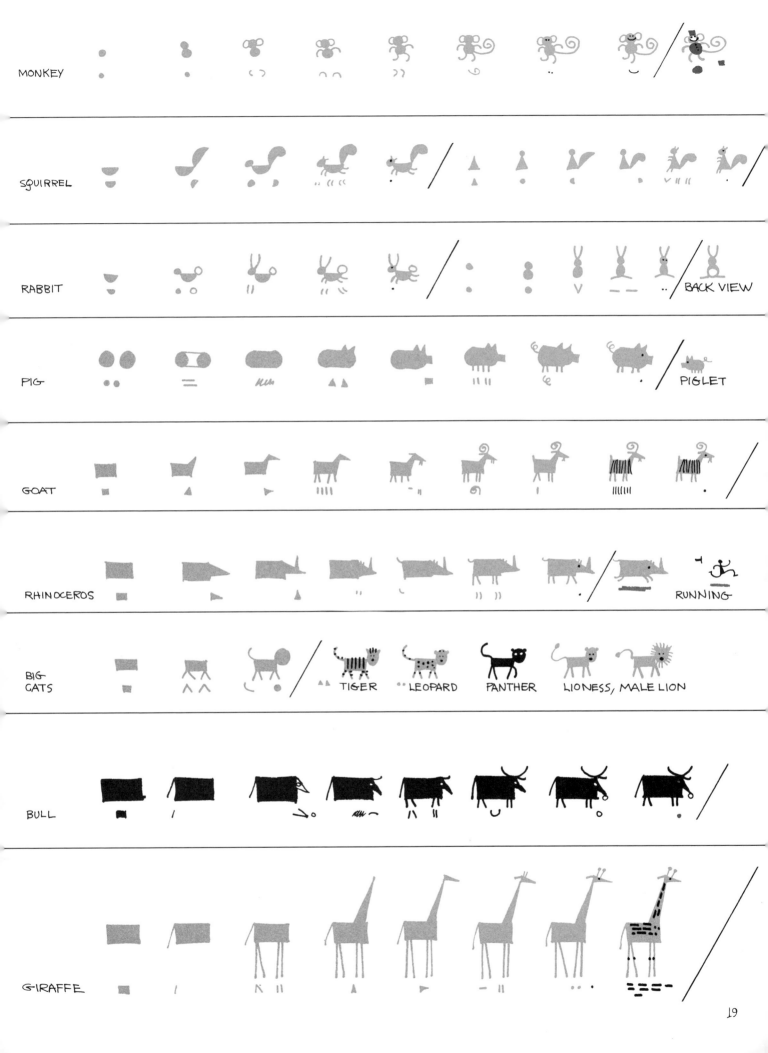

MONKEY

SQUIRREL

RABBIT — BACK VIEW

PIG — PIGLET

GOAT

RHINOCEROS — RUNNING

BIG CATS — TIGER   LEOPARD   PANTHER   LIONESS, MALE LION

BULL

GIRAFFE

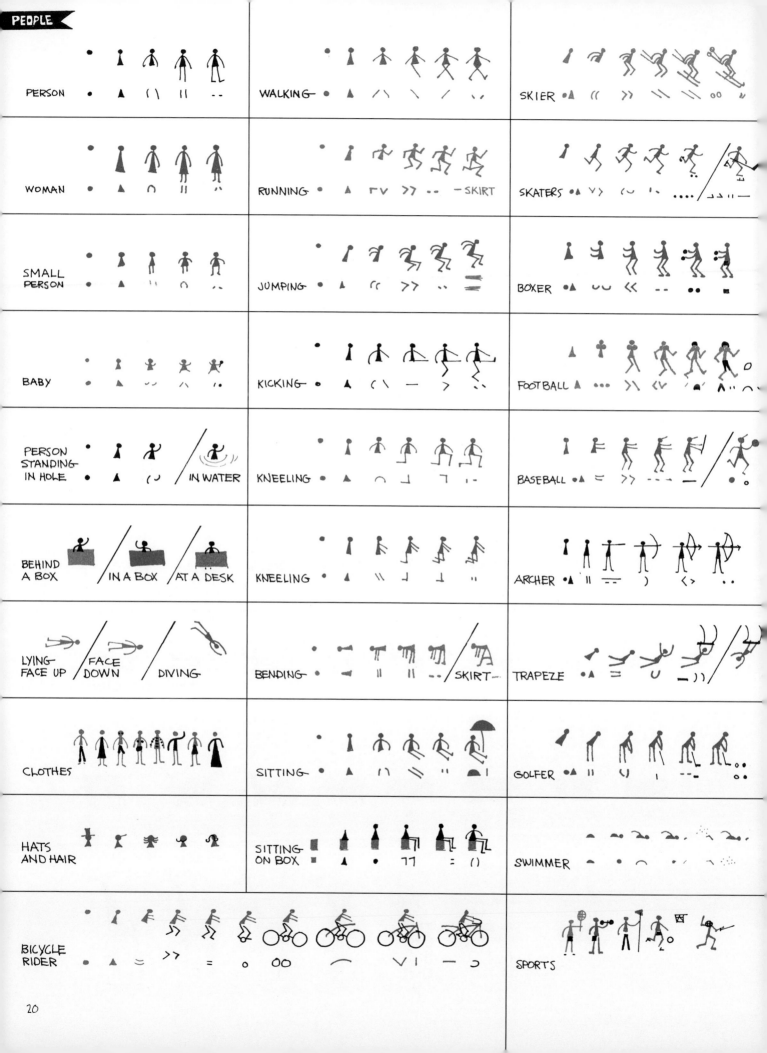

PERSON

WOMAN

SMALL PERSON

BABY

PERSON STANDING IN HOLE / IN WATER

BEHIND A BOX / IN A BOX / AT A DESK

LYING FACE UP / FACE DOWN / DIVING

CLOTHES

HATS AND HAIR

BICYCLE RIDER

WALKING

RUNNING

JUMPING

KICKING

KNEELING

KNEELING

BENDING / SKIRT

SITTING

SITTING ON BOX

SKIER

SKATERS

BOXER

FOOTBALL

BASEBALL

ARCHER

TRAPEZE

GOLFER

SWIMMER

SPORTS

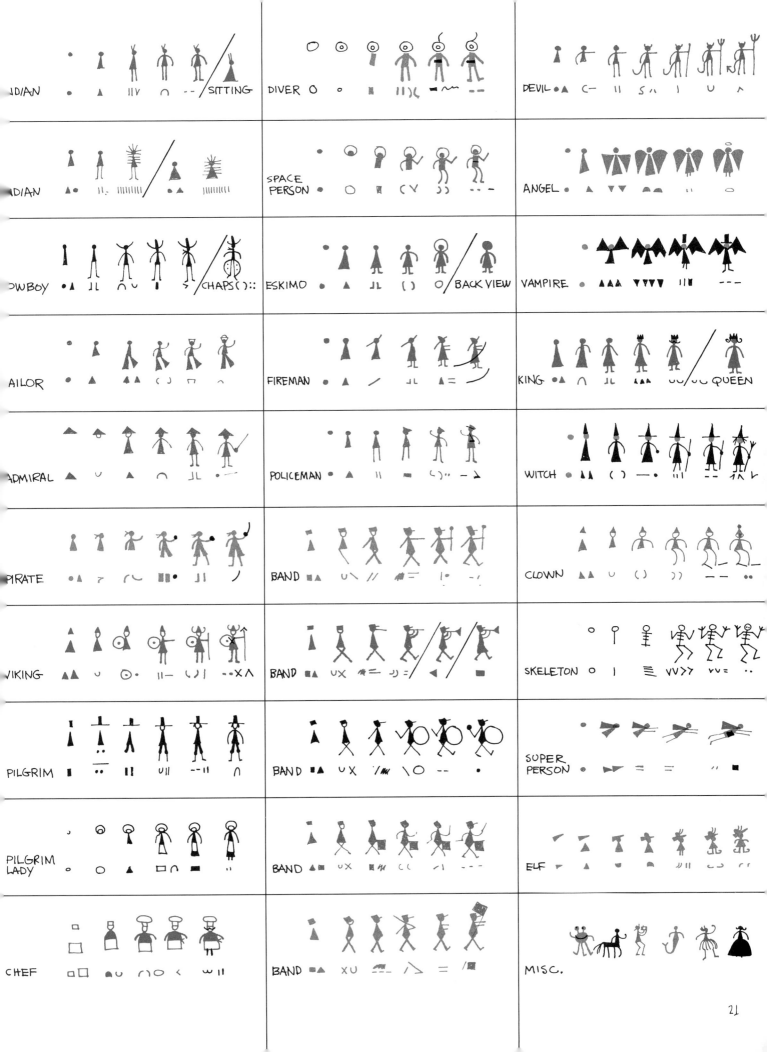

NDIAN ... SITTING

NDIAN

OWBOY ... CHAPS( )::

AILOR

ADMIRAL

PIRATE

VIKING

PILGRIM

PILGRIM LADY

CHEF

DIVER

SPACE PERSON

ESKIMO ... BACK VIEW

FIREMAN

POLICEMAN

BAND

BAND

BAND

BAND

BAND

DEVIL

ANGEL

VAMPIRE

KING ... QUEEN

WITCH

CLOWN

SKELETON

SUPER PERSON

ELF

MISC.

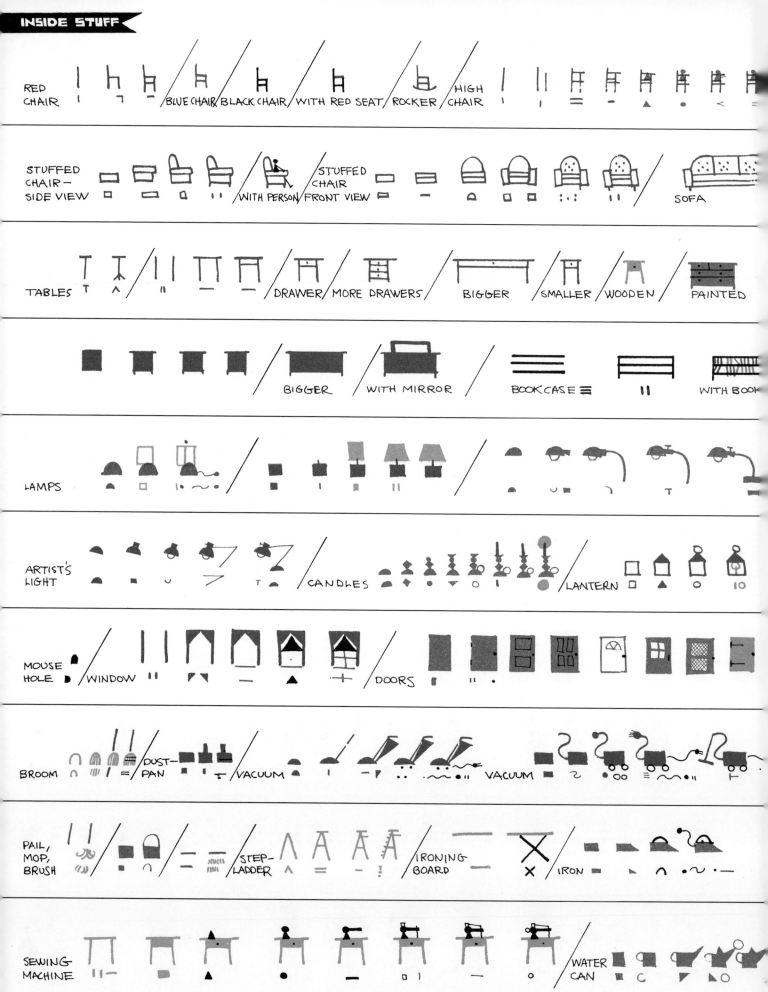

RED CHAIR

BLUE CHAIR / BLACK CHAIR / WITH RED SEAT / ROCKER / HIGH CHAIR

STUFFED CHAIR – SIDE VIEW

WITH PERSON / STUFFED CHAIR FRONT VIEW

SOFA

TABLES

DRAWER / MORE DRAWERS / BIGGER / SMALLER / WOODEN / PAINTED

BIGGER / WITH MIRROR / BOOKCASE / WITH BOOK

LAMPS

ARTIST'S LIGHT / CANDLES / LANTERN

MOUSE HOLE / WINDOW / DOORS

BROOM / DUSTPAN / VACUUM / VACUUM

PAIL, MOP, BRUSH / STEP-LADDER / IRONING BOARD / IRON

SEWING MACHINE / WATER CAN

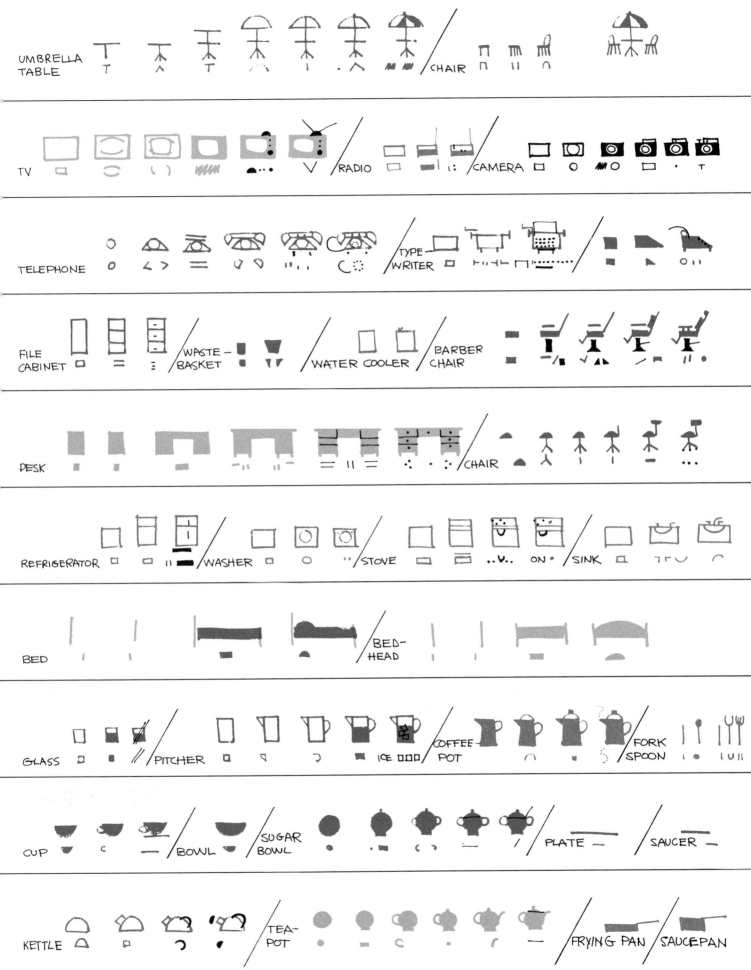

UMBRELLA TABLE / CHAIR

TV / RADIO / CAMERA

TELEPHONE / TYPE-WRITER

FILE CABINET / WASTE-BASKET / WATER COOLER / BARBER CHAIR

DESK / CHAIR

REFRIGERATOR / WASHER / STOVE / SINK

BED / BED-HEAD

GLASS / PITCHER / ICE / COFFEE-POT / FORK SPOON

CUP / BOWL / SUGAR BOWL / PLATE / SAUCER

KETTLE / TEA-POT / FRYING PAN / SAUCEPAN

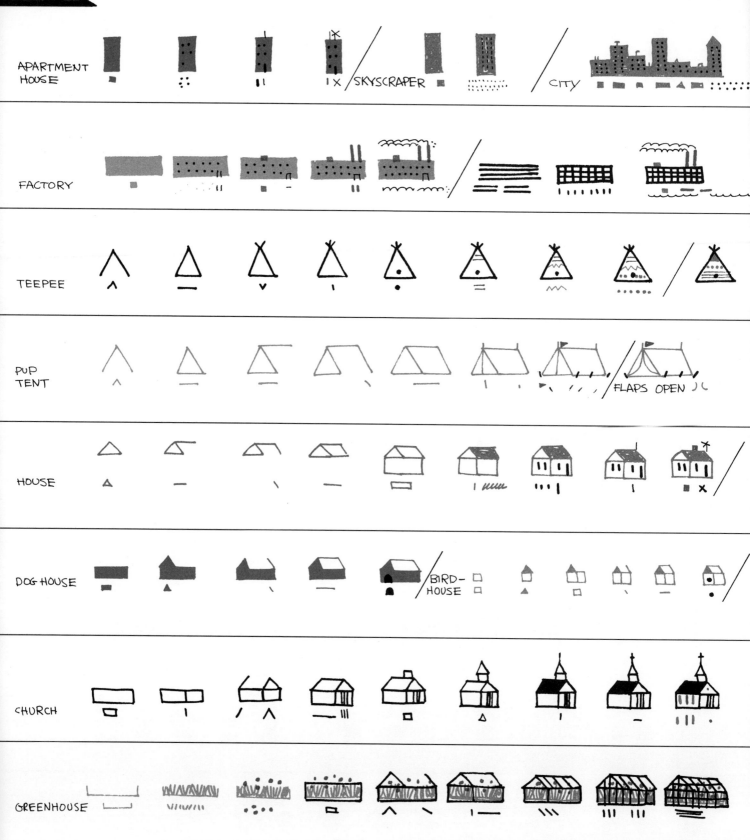

APARTMENT HOUSE / SKYSCRAPER / CITY

FACTORY

TEEPEE

PUP TENT / FLAPS OPEN

HOUSE

DOG HOUSE / BIRD-HOUSE

CHURCH

GREENHOUSE

CASTLE

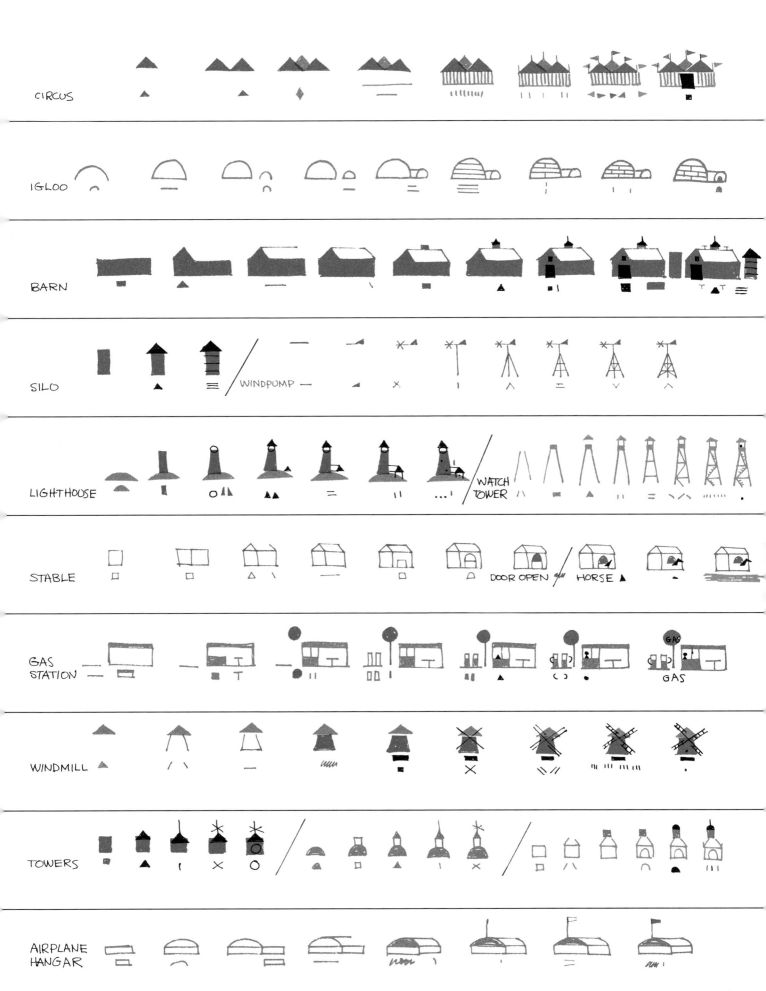

CIRCUS

IGLOO

BARN

SILO

WINDPUMP

LIGHTHOUSE

WATCH TOWER

STABLE

DOOR OPEN

HORSE

GAS STATION

GAS

WINDMILL

TOWERS

AIRPLANE HANGAR

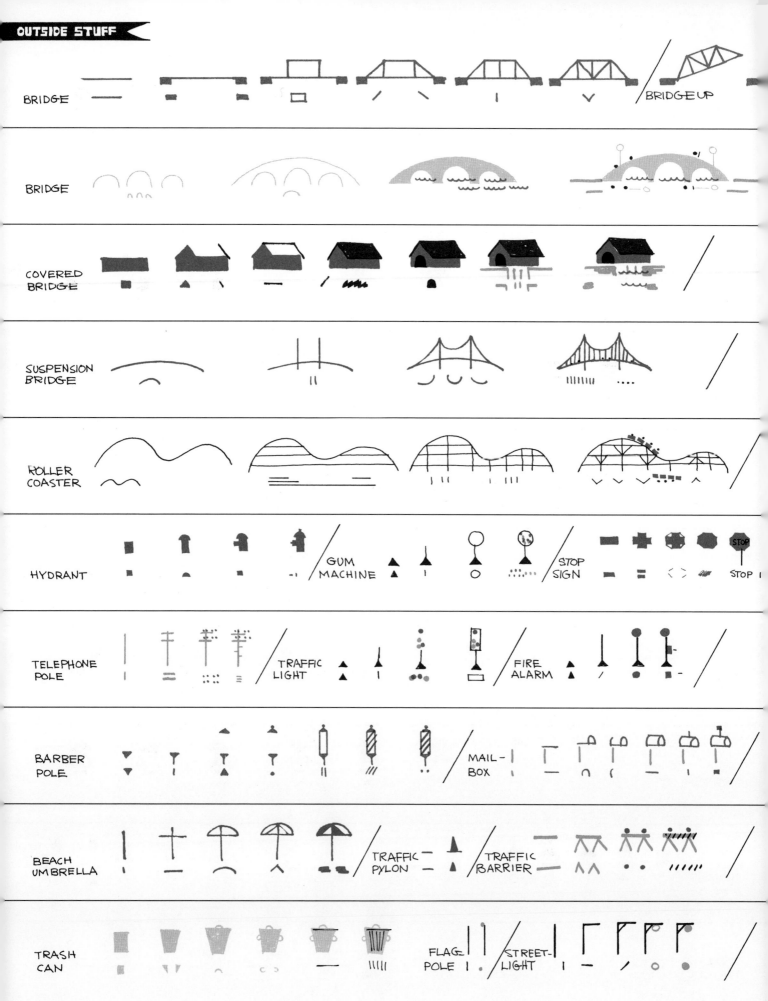

BRIDGE

BRIDGE UP

BRIDGE

COVERED BRIDGE

SUSPENSION BRIDGE

ROLLER COASTER

HYDRANT

GUM MACHINE

STOP SIGN

STOP

TELEPHONE POLE

TRAFFIC LIGHT

FIRE ALARM

BARBER POLE

MAIL-BOX

BEACH UMBRELLA

TRAFFIC PYLON

TRAFFIC BARRIER

TRASH CAN

FLAG-POLE

STREET-LIGHT

26

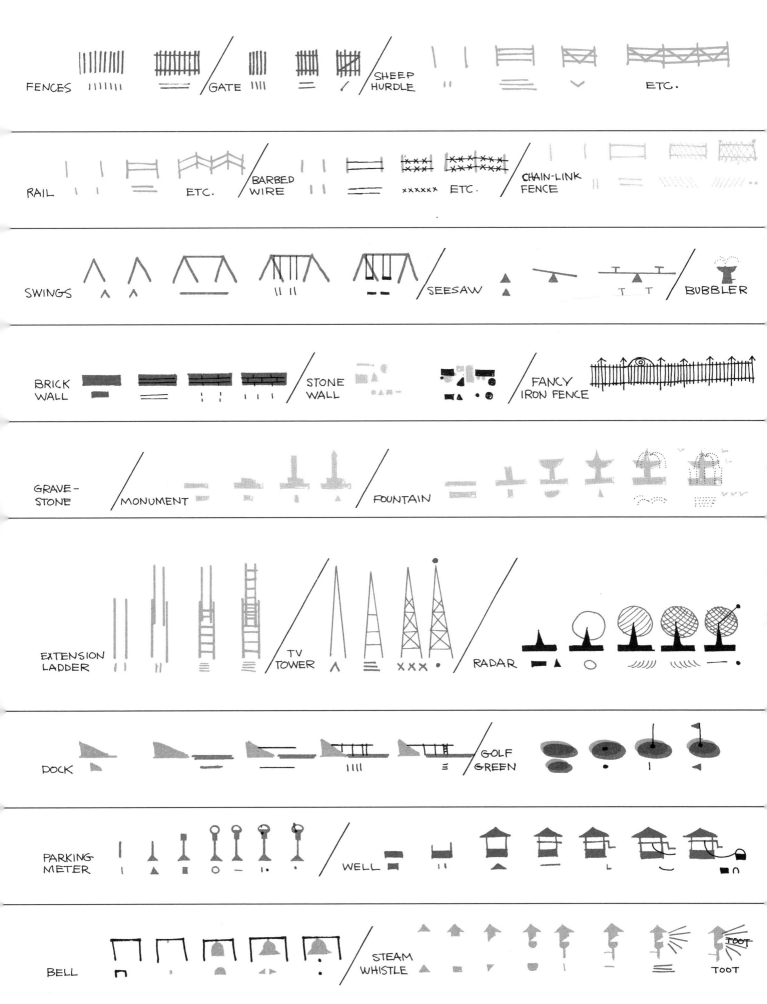

FENCES

GATE

SHEEP HURDLE

ETC.

RAIL

ETC.

BARBED WIRE

ETC.

CHAIN-LINK FENCE

SWINGS

SEESAW

BUBBLER

BRICK WALL

STONE WALL

FANCY IRON FENCE

GRAVE-STONE

MONUMENT

FOUNTAIN

EXTENSION LADDER

TV TOWER

RADAR

DOCK

GOLF GREEN

PARKING METER

WELL

BELL

STEAM WHISTLE

TOOT

TOOT

27

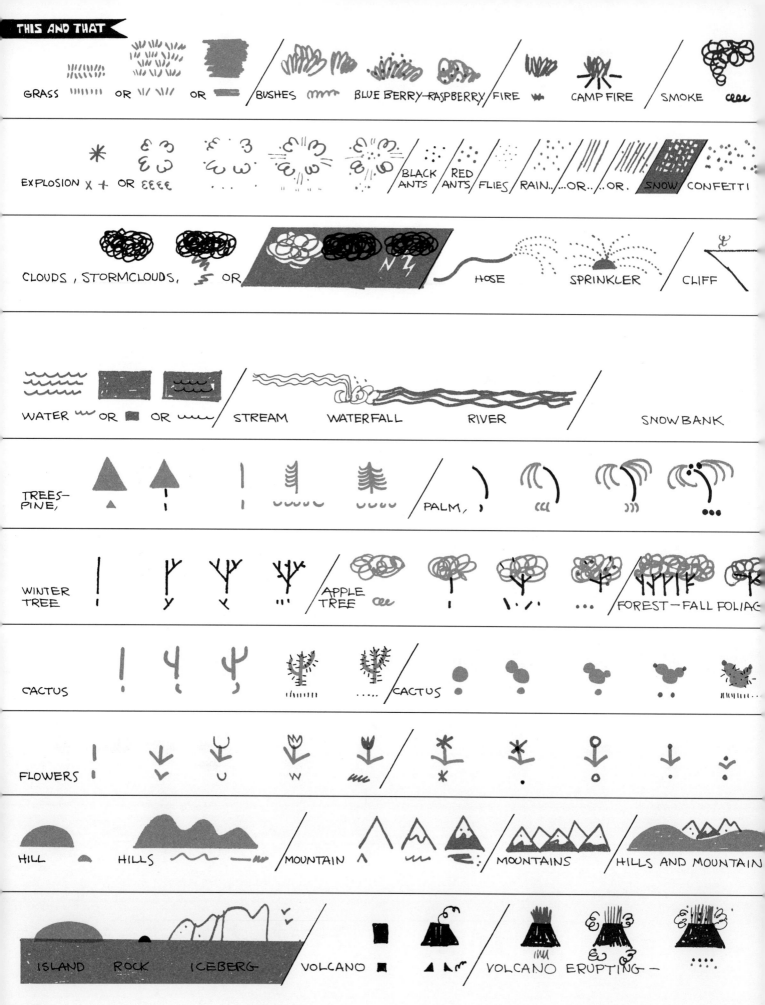

GRASS   OR   OR   / BUSHES   BLUE BERRY–RASPBERRY   FIRE   CAMP FIRE   / SMOKE

EXPLOSION X + OR Ɛ3Ɛ3   BLACK ANTS / RED ANTS / FLIES / RAIN...OR......OR.. SNOW CONFETTI

CLOUDS , STORMCLOUDS,   OR   HOSE   SPRINKLER   / CLIFF

WATER   OR   OR   / STREAM   WATERFALL   RIVER   / SNOWBANK

TREES– PINE,   PALM,

WINTER TREE   APPLE TREE   FOREST—FALL FOLIAGE

CACTUS   CACTUS

FLOWERS

HILL   HILLS   / MOUNTAIN   MOUNTAINS   / HILLS AND MOUNTAIN

ISLAND   ROCK   ICEBERG   / VOLCANO   VOLCANO ERUPTING—

KITE     **BALLOONS**

PIRATE CANNON

PIRATE FLAG

BRITISH FLAG   1620 1776

CANADIAN FLAG

AMERICAN FLAG    **WAVING**

OTHER FLAGS

FRANCE — ITALY — ICELAND — FINLAND — JAPAN — HUNGARY — CZECHOSLOVAKIA — NIGERIA — COSTA RICA —

THIS AND THAT

BIRTHDAY CAKE — FIRECRACKER — CAMERA — SLINGSHOT — BIRDS ——— BUTTERFLIES — HOLE — PLANET —

¾ VIEW OF CAR   **BACK VIEW**

FACES: HAPPY, ANGRY, SLY, SAD, SHY, LAUGHING, CRYING, SHOUTING, SINGING

✳ HERE ARE SOME OF THE THINGS
YOU CAN DO WITH YOUR PICTURES...

COMIC STRIPS...

POSTERS...

PATTERNS...   BORDERS...

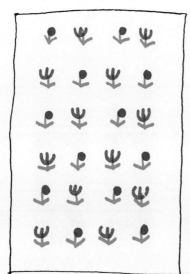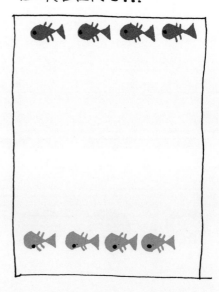

BOOKS....

MOBILES...

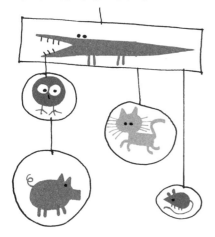

SIGNS...

CARDS...

LETTERS...

GAMES, ETC...

＊THERE ARE MANY WAYS
THE DRAWINGS IN THIS BOOK AND YOUR OWN DRAWINGS
CAN BE PUT TOGETHER, ADDED TO OR CHANGED
TO MAKE SOME WORLDS OF YOUR OWN.
FOR INSTANCE...